The Cyber Threat
And The Role of Cyber Intelligence In Defending Your Organization

Bob Gourley

CONTENTS

1   Know The Cyber Threat   1

2   Who Is Attacking   5

3   Trends From History   11

4   Adversary Tactics   19

5   Enhancing Your Intelligence Efforts   27

6   Architect To Win   35

7   Cyber Intelligence Feeds   41

8   A Strategic Assessment   47

9   Concluding Thoughts   59

10 Appendix 1: The History   65

11 Appendix 2: Sources   83

12 About the Author   91

13 Acknowledgements   93

Know The Cyber Threat

"There are no excuses anymore. Trying to run a business without awareness of the cyber threat is asking to be fired."
Scott McNealy

You might want to know the cyber threat out of curiosity. Or maybe you want to dive into it for entertainment; there are thrilling stories to tell here. But if you are in business there are other, mission critical reasons to study the threat.

Business leaders study the cyber threat because of a need to avoid operational and financial losses, meet regulatory requirements, mitigate liability, protect sensitive corporate and client information from unauthorized disclosure or destruction, avoid business disruption, protect brands and maintain reputation. Knowing the threat, and establishing intelligence driven defenses, will make direct contributions to protecting your business. Conversely, ignoring the threat can put your business in peril.

Leaders study the threat to beat the threat. And as tough as the threats are, one thing is clear, they can be beat. Sometimes you will beat them before they breach, sometimes after they breach. But they can definitely be beat.

You can be beat too. But your interest in this subject probably means you have already learned that the hard way. You probably also already concluded your organization will win more if you arm yourself with knowledge of what you are up against.

The threats will evolve, so keep in mind your study needs to be a continuous activity. And mechanisms can be put in place in your organization that keep the right decision-makers informed of the nature of the threat. The art and science of this approach is called Cyber Threat Intelligence.

Expect Informed Insights

This review provides a high level overview of cyber threats to business interests, discusses the important lessons history can teach us regarding the threat, and then provides actionable suggestions on ways to enhance your organization's cyber intelligence operations.

The information here is based on decades of experience tracking the cyber threat. At Cognitio we work with a wide range of organizations in multiple sectors of the economy and in government and have seen first hand the struggle organizations are in to defend their businesses against the cyber threat.

One thing we see again and again is how important awareness of the threat is to mounting an effective defense. Additionally, we see too frequently that even when some parts of an organization have a respect for the cyber threat, others parts do not and that can weaken defense. Organizations, especially large ones, need better shared threat awareness.

The lessons we provide here flow from a mix of first-hand experience, as well as the open studies and assessments we publish online at our CTOvision.com blog, the daily threat reports published at our ThreatBrief.com site, the published research of leading cyber security firms, and open reporting by governments and law enforcement organizations. We also draw on research and work of non-profits including the Cyber Conflict Studies Association (CCSA) and the Intelligence and National Security Alliance (INSA). The community of incident response centers and academic research from the highly regarded computer security activities of Purdue University and Carnegie Mellon University were also key sources of material. Other sources include a network of associates we have worked with since the late 1990's who graciously agreed to review this report and offer views and perspectives from their direct experience in working to mitigate threats.

For further study we provide a list of key references in the Sources and Methods Appendix of the report. Links to these references are all available in a comprehensive reference at our site at TheCyberThreat.com.

Who Is Attacking?

A widely-used taxonomy breaks threat actors into:

- National Governments
- Industrial Spies and Organized Crime Groups
- Terrorists and Extremist Groups
- Hackers and Hacktivists
- Trusted Insiders

This taxonomy is helpful in thinking through actions to take before and during attacks since the nature of attacks by these actors will be different.

National Governments:

In 2013 the cyber security firm Mandiant published a report outlining what many had assumed was occurring but could now see as fact: the Chinese government was supporting a systematic program of cyber espionage, euphemistically termed the "Advanced Persistent Threat", targeting over 140 companies in 20 major industries. Reporting through 2013 and 2014 implied that Russia has sanctioned attacks against firms in Europe and on Wall Street as responses to U.S. and NATO opposition to Russian activities in the Ukraine. Iran has been accused of penetrating infrastructures to prepare for offensive attacks, and in December 2014 the FBI officially attributed attacks against Sony to the DPRK.

If a country has decided attack you then they have made a decision that they will not quickly change and they will have resources, time and patience. The only way you will beat this nationally-sponsored adversary is by involving a broad community that should include law enforcement, community consortia (like the appropriate information sharing and analysis center (ISAC) for your sector, as well as specialized security researchers and cyber intelligence firms. You will want to raise your defenses and present a harder target but do not make the mistake of thinking you can defend against these players by yourself or with static defenses.

Industrial Spies and Organized Crime:

The recent and well-publicized attacks against Target, Home Depot, and Anthem are probably the work of sophisticated criminal organizations, but this category contains many different actors with different objectives. In 2015 the FBI reported there are over 60 major cyber crime groups linked to nation-states, so at times this element blends with the nation state level attacker.

There are so many criminal groups that attacks occur continuously. How you respond depends on what you know of who is attacking, making cyber intelligence especially important against this type of actor. If you can capture data of forensic value then law enforcement might be able to help. You may be able to mitigate this level of attack with well-led cyber security activities, but the resources of these bad actors means they will likely achieve some success against you. Early detection is key here, with statistics indicating most criminals get inside enterprises in a matter of minutes or hours and most defenders not noticing them for months. The nature of this threat means you must be prepared for response when they breach.

Terrorists and Extremists Groups:

If you are under attack from these groups in cyberspace you should also be concerned with physical attacks perhaps timed with key public events. Connections between physical and cyber security are likely of growing importance.

Hackers and Hacktivists:

Attacks from this category of actor occur continuously. Hacktivist groups with geo-political/social agendas (e.g., Anonymous, Lulzsec, AntiSec, etc) are here to stay. These groups are looking for publicity and the reputational risk they pose to your organization can be huge. Organizations with solid defenses and good cyber intelligence stand a chance of keeping these attackers out, but the complexity of modern enterprises and the number of vectors these attackers can use indicate you would be wise to prepare to respond to breach.

The Insider Threat:

The term "Insider Threat" has a special use in the cyber security community. It is used to describe a person operating in your organization who is legitimate-yet-malicious. At times this term is also applied to the totally innocent insider with good intentions who is duped into operating for others, perhaps by clicking a link or visiting a website with malicious code. Once this is done, valid, insider credentials can be extracted for use by outsiders, blurring this distinction in this category.

This aspect of the insider threat make it a particularly dangerous one. It is so significant that leaders in the intelligence community have been calling this the greatest potential threat for decades. The prescience of this assessment came true in what would be the greatest cyber attack against the intelligence community to date; the insider attacks by Edward Snowden in the summer of 2013.

Expanding This Assessment

We provide more information on attack methodologies used by all threat actors (internal and external to the enterprise) and suggestions for ways to mitigate key elements of the threat in coming sections. We will provide a forward looking threat assessment on the cyber threat from nations, criminals, extremists and hackers after a review of their attack patterns and the history of the threat.

Table One: Who Attacks?

Actor	Motive	Targets
Governments	Economic or Military	IP or infrastructure
Organized Crime	Financial gain	Bank or investment information or IP
Extremists	Support to causes	Highly visible targets, information to enable other attacks
Hackers and Hacktivists	Glory, support to causes	Any soft target

Trends From Cyber History

People have been conducting attacks on, in and through communications systems for a very long time. But there are elements of our interconnected technology systems and attacks in them that can be very hard to understand. Perhaps this is because our senses cannot directly observe what happens in our computer systems. Perceiving this environment is much harder than understanding the physical world we evolved in, and this lack of perception contributes to a tendency for organizations to forget history, forget attacks and discount threats. We call this tendency for organizations to forget the cyber threat "Cyber Threat Amnesia." There is only one way to really defeat cyber threat amnesia-- through study of history.

Where Does Cyber History Start?

Cyber history is older than you may think. Both sides in the U.S. Civil War attacked telegraph lines of the other, and there are examples of missions being conducted to insert false orders into adversary communications. Every war since has demonstrated that when an adversary wants to use information and information technology as a weapon, they will and with great effect. We also see again and again that agility in defense is key. An ability to change configurations to protect is important. A moving target is hard to hit.

What Should I Know About Cyber History?

Every executive in industry and leader in government should know this point: History underscores again and again that the threat is dynamic. If an adversary has an objective that can be accomplished by attacking via computers they will attack and will alter their attack to succeed.

Another key point from history, especially modern history, is that cybercrime happens continuously. We might study episodic events, but the attackers are operating non-stop.

Decision-makers with a more direct role in protecting systems would be well served by having a deeper familiarity with the history of the cyber threat and the many related lessons it offers. Understanding our shared history gives us a common baseline for discussing and understanding threat behaviors and helps ingrain lessons learned.

Appendix 1 outlines a brief history of significant cyber-history events. We summarize some of the most famous events and executive level lessons in Table Two below.

Table Two: Key Points in History

Event	Summary	Executive Lesson
1986 Hanover Hacker	Espionage	Prepare for Collaboration
2007/8 Estonia + Georgia	Attackers supporting Russian objectives	Cyber attacks are now part of all International Conflicts
2009 GhostNet	Large scale espionage	Nothing will stop an adversary that wants to get in. Prepare for a breach
2011 ShadyRAT	Economic espionage	Collaborative work gets results
2013 Manidant Report	Economic espionage	Collaboration for strategic use is key
2014 Retail Attacks	Almost daily news of cyber attacks	Prepare to mitigate risks, but prepare to respond to breach
2014 Operation Cleaver	Iran preparing for strategic attack	Nations will use cyber as strategic weapons
2014 Sony Attacks	Blended attacks by DPRK and Hackers	Have your response plan in place prior to attack

Key points from this review of history:

If history does not exactly repeat itself, it most certainly echoes. In too many cases, organizations were surprised when they were attacked. Organizations can mitigate some of that unwarranted surprise by enhancing intelligence activities, because the threat will not go away and it will constantly innovate.

Defenders innovate too, and history has its share of success in defending against the threat. But every defense can eventually be penetrated. Defense must continue to improve. One way of doing that is for defenders to learn to think more like the attacker. Learn about the threat.

Another clear lesson comes from successes in defeating adversaries: knowing who is attacking can help since it can lead to assessments on the attack paths they will likely chose and can help inform operational and tactical responses.

As this report is being written we are on the cusp of another paradigm shifting change in technology architectures. Cyber and physical systems are being mashed up together to create new architectures more complex than ever. Lessons from history will no doubt be relevant, but we must apply them to increasingly complex, interconnected environments that include cloud computing, more use of consumer technologies in enterprise environments, mobile devices, wearable/drivable/flyable computers, drones and an incredible amount of Internet connected sensors. Adding to the seriousness of the threat in this new architecture, there are few emerging standards supportive of security or authentication or authorization.

History tells us that adversaries will always seek to exploit the technology, and our technology is about to connect to everything we have. Imagine an adversary exploiting a flaw in your home lawn sprinkler and from there leaping into your toaster and then your watch to steal your work login and then leaping into your office computer. Security researchers have already proven that attacks against medical devices, even pacemakers, insulin pumps and other devices, are possible. Automobiles have also been hacked and proven attacks exist that could contribute to accidents. This might sound like a bad science fiction movie, but the trends of technology and lessons of history say this is the world of the near future.

Adversary Tactics

Cybersecurity professionals study adversary tactics so defenses can be strengthened prior to attack and so clues can be developed while under attack that might lead to estimates of the bad guy's next move. Business leaders should study adversary tactics to understand the reality of the threat. This can help inform risk decisions and help in your dialog with other business professionals.

Every year for the last ten years Verizon has worked collegially across a broad range of organizations to analyze successful intrusions into enterprises. The results of this analysis is published in an annual Data Breach Investigations Report.

The 2014 Verizon Data Breach Investigations Report was particularly insightful when it comes to describing how adversaries are getting into systems. Researchers concluded that all known attacks could be categorized into common attack patterns. Their methodology was tested against 10 years of breach data, resulting in historical proof that these patterns describe key adversary behaviors that defenders must prepare to mitigate.

The attack patterns are:

- Cyber Espionage
- Web application attacks
- Crimeware
- Insider Misuse
- Errors and their exploitation
- Physical Theft
- Denial of Service attacks
- Point of Sale and Payment Card attacks

Here is more on each of these patterns:

Cyber Espionage: These are attacks that include unauthorized access to steal information. Increasingly these are by state-sponsored actors that exhibit the motive of espionage. This type of attack is also conducted by criminal groups for financial motive. As a category of breach this method has been growing consistently and exhibits a wider range of threat actions than any other pattern, meaning the adversary here will do what ever it takes to get in and get your information out.

Web application attacks: This category

includes any incident where a web application was the vector of attack, including exploits of code-level vulnerabilities in the application and also attacks that thwart authentication mechanisms. Most incidents were due to a weakness in the application or by using stolen credentials. Many recent attacks are designed to gain control of servers, including conducting flooding attacks on others or for defacing the websites. Some attacks are launched as part of a campaign to get other information that can be used for escalating cyber intelligence attacks.

Crimeware: This attack pattern describes incidents that are led by the use of malicious software. The primary goal is to gain control of a system as a platform for illicit use such as stealing credentials, spamming or information theft. Web downloads and attacks targeting unsuspecting users are the most common infection vector. Very frequently this method of attack starts with an outside attacker tricking an insider in an enterprise into clicking a link (a phishing or spearphishing attack) or they find they can get malicious code into the enterprise by planting it on a website that has a high likelihood of being viewed by a particular target (a watering hole attack). This first entry is then used for escalated attacks.

Insider Misuse: This is a broad category, which includes any unapproved or malicious use of organizational resources. Describing insider activities must take into account assistance of outsiders (collusion) and partners on the inside that may be unwitting. Most crimes of this sort are conducted for financial or personal gain, with others being conducted by disgruntled employees or for ideological reasons. This includes targeting internal data and trade secrets.

Errors and their exploitation: This category of incident involved exploiting unintentional actions on the part of the technology team. This is especially exploited where highly repetitive and mundane business processes are required.

Physical Theft: Critical to track and mitigate since physical theft can cause mission-impacting harm and can also lead to compromised credentials and other information that can lead to escalating attacks. In most cases assets are stolen from corporate offices.

Denial of Service attacks: These are attacks intended to compromise the availability of networks and systems. Includes both network and application layer attacks. There are cases where massive denial of service attacks are conducted to distract responders to other more low key attacks underway at the same time.

Point of Sale and Payment Card intrusions: Remote attacks against the environments where retail transactions are conducted, specifically where card-present purchases are made. Can involve physically implanting devices that read magnetic stripe data. The number of big name breaches in these categories is clearly on the rise. A resurgence of malicious software that operates in memory (RAM) is a prominent tactical development that will inform other attack vectors.

Table Three: Attack Patterns

Method	Summary	Executive Lesson
Espionage Methods	Human guided tools to find and extract information	Prioritize, classify and protect your data
Web Application Attacks	Try every way to break into a website or application	Do not host websites, keep them off your networks
Malicious Code	Virus, worms and other bad code that can at times replicate	Automate detection and response is key
Exploit Poor Configuration	Adversaries seek any mistake to exploit	Put leaders in charge who can reduce attack surface
Point of Sales and Payment Card	Criminals will always find ways to exploit financial transactions	Ensure that you have access to tactical threat intelligence

A key takeaway from this discussion:

It goes without saying that these many attack patterns can be mixed, and the more resources an adversary has the more likely that multiple strategies will be tried against you. Optimal defenses vary from attack pattern to attack pattern, so positioning your defenses should be informed by what you know of your own business, your own systems, and the priority targets you present to adversaries.

You will be attacked. What matters the most is how you deal with the inevitable.

Enhancing Intelligence Efforts

Intelligence professionals look at intelligence in three levels: Strategic, Operational and Tactical. This framework also applies to businesses developing an intelligence capability. It is the best way to ensure the right allocation of required resources to accomplish your intelligence objectives.

We offer definitions of these levels of cyber intelligence below, and will then return to this construct to discuss decisions this type of intelligence supports and steps that can be taken to enhance cyber intelligence at each level.

Strategic Cyber Intelligence:

Analysis and information that can help organizations understand the type of threat they are architecting against, the motivation and capability of the threat actor as well as the potential impacts. This information allows effective planning for the resources to protect against and mitigate current and future threats. The information at this level should be evidence based but can also include informed projections on what could be, including potential future courses of actions of adversaries and what they might do once your future architectures (including mobile, cloud or other) are in place.

Operational Cyber Intelligence:

Information that can inform your day-to-day decision-making, resource allocation and task prioritization. It includes trend analysis showing the technical direction of adversaries, indications that an adversary has selected a particular target and revelations of adversary tactics, techniques and procedures. It can also be information useful to identifying the threat including the threat active against your networks.

Tactical Cyber Intelligence:

Information coming from direct adversary action inside your systems or from other sources that have the potential to immediately inform your tactical decisions. This information is typically derived from real-time monitoring of systems or from other real-time information sharing.

Intelligence Drives Decisions

Information on the threat informs different decisions at different levels. Ensuring you have the right information on the threat at each level can significantly improve your ability to defend your organization. The conclusions intelligence analysis will develop will vary from situation to situation, but we provide some key use cases below as food for thought.

Strategic Decisions:

Strategic threat intelligence can be of critical importance in building support for the resources you will need to build a strong defense. Strategic intelligence might come in the form of threat briefings tailored to your industry or your organization. After receiving threat briefs you may decide to change the way you track cyber threats as a risk, or perhaps request reprioritization of your current IT spend to enhance cyber security, or perhaps build the case for new cyber security funding.

You can also use strategic intelligence to help build the case for stronger coordination and collaboration with other organizations. Enhanced and more accurate strategic cyber intelligence will help you structure your internal organization to make you more able to respond to threats.

Strategic intelligence will help your organization understand the degree of agility that will be needed in mounting defenses against fast moving adversaries.

You should also use strategic information to plan for exercise and training programs for your cyber security and IT staff, as well as for executives in your organization who will need to respond to ongoing operational situations. Strategic decisions will also include how you prioritize your system control efforts (for example, prioritizing controls based on ISO or NIST or similar standards). In most cases, good strategic intelligence will motivate enterprises to relook processes. This should include both non-technical processes like audit, and technical processes like configuration management to reduce IT errors.

Operational Decisions:

The operational decisions made by security professionals, IT teams and even executives will be better informed when you know which tools adversaries are using, which vulnerabilities they are exploiting, and what techniques other defenders are using to successfully mitigate the threat.

This will enable better decisions on daily work schedules and prioritization as well as choices on who you collaborate with for collective defense and how to collaborate. Other operational decisions include the policies you put into your IT systems for automated response to tactical threats.

Tactical Decisions:

Better tactical intelligence can lead to conclusions on what adversaries want which can help you make rapid decisions on what to block, what to allow, and at times what to shut down. Unfortunately, lack of tactical intelligence often leads to businesses making the wrong decisions, resulting in either adversaries getting all the information they want or key services being taken offline. Better tactical intelligence can ensure these decisions are optimized. Increasingly organizations are putting automated policies in place to enable tactical information to result in automated responses. This is a great use of tactical intelligence. But this approach is only made possible when good strategic and operational intelligence are also optimized. All of this needs to come together to enable operation at network speed.

By optimizing intelligence at each of these levels the quality of decisions can be improved. This can become a particularly virtuous cycle since using good intelligence will motivate more tasking and use of good intelligence. An example of how this virtuous cycle can improve security posture is in the way predictive cyber intelligence can enhance threat modeling which can inform security vulnerability and penetration testing to improve security posture, and all the lessons from this can then inform additional assessments.

Table Four: Levels of Cyber Intelligence Support

Level	Summary	Executive Lesson
Strategic	Supports highest levels of organization. Includes support to risk management	Ensure all business leaders know the threat
Operational	Supports day-to-day business decisions. Includes indications of impending attack	Much will be provided from outside the organization. Architect for success now
Tactical	Serving cyber defenders making real time decisions to mitigate threats	Sources include own nets plus outside sources

Architect to Enhance Your Intelligence

Optimize Your Intelligence Information At All Three Levels

Intelligence support to cyber operations should be treated as a discipline with forethought put into how you will acquire the right intelligence at every level. How this is done will vary from organization to organization, but some overall guiding thoughts can help you kick start your cyber intelligence operation.

Architect for Strategic Cyber Intelligence:

We strongly recommend that every enterprise track the strategic threat and take steps to ensure that all stakeholders are aware of the strategic cyber threat. There are many open/public references available to do this, including government reports and reporting from the major cyber security vendors. It also pays to reach out to representatives of your industry that track cyber threats (including the sector Information Sharing and Analysis Centers (ISACs) if appropriate for your industry). Establish a relationship with your closest FBI field office and inquire of strategic threat briefings from them. Their views on the threat can inform your ability to architect for a defense.

Architect for Operational Cyber Intelligence:

The community of cyber emergency response teams (CERTs) is very likely already known by many in your organization. Consider whether you are taking full advantage of this type of important community information. There are also sources of operational cyber intelligence curated by the Department of Homeland Security, including information from the US-CERT. The Defense Cyber Crime Center (DC3) also provides important, daily context. We also recommend the daily context provided by the SANS organization (SANS Newsbytes). There are also many paid sources of operational cyber intelligence including many which can be purchased as part of managed security offerings, some of which we review below.

As important as your sources of operational information is how your organization will analyze and act upon it. The function of staying on top of these important flows of threat information should be assigned to a small group with the ability to glean the most relevant insights from them.

Architect for Tactical Cyber Intelligence:

Architecting for intelligence at the tactical level requires the most attention to automation. Tactical cyber intelligence works best when highly automated. Low degrees of automation require high degrees of human analysis and that slows decision time and gives adversaries the advantage. Some organizations put in place automated means to hunt for bad actors in their networks. This can be a terrific source of tactical cyber intelligence.

Sources of information can include external feeds from the Computer Emergency Response Team (CERT) community and from other related technical sources, but critical information is going to come from your own networks and computers. Information can be collected on adversary action before breach that can reveal key characteristics of the adversary and their methods and at times lead to conclusions about what their intentions are. During a breach, tactical information can help you block data exfiltration while helping to push the adversary out. When done well, tactical intelligence can lead to automated removal of threats.

A key capability in this area is a robust and effective incident response program that is integrated into the business environment. In addition, the cyber incident response capability should be exercised regularly. Remember, you don't want to be exchanging business cards during the crisis. The response team should include all aspects of the business, not just IT or security.

Architecting for tactical cyber intelligence should also include establishing secure collaborative environments for your own cyber security team plus secure means to collaborate with other defenders in your sector and throughout the cyber security community. Secure information sharing and collaboration does not just happen, it takes forethought and planning.

A Final Note on Architecting To Win:

Optimizing intelligence at strategic, operational and tactical levels requires a plan and leadership.

Identifying the leader responsible for designing, building and operationalizing this intelligence architecture and ensuring it is relevant in the business/mission context is perhaps the most important step in the process. As you architect, understand that since it is impossible to protect everything at the same level, you need a mature enterprise risk management capability to identify what must be protected with the highest levels of defense. Cyber intelligence will support this risk-based methodology and knowing the business will also inform your priorities for cyber intelligence.

Table Five: Architect To Win

Level	Summary
Strategic	Put someone in command. Establish relationships with external organizations that can provide cyber intelligence. Evaluate cyber threats in context of enterprise risk management and audit
Operational	Engineer the right data feeds and threat advisories. Ensure business leaders have relevant information provided
Tactical	Ensure technical team is on path to automate everything that can be automated, especially incident data, but also response and remediation

Cyber Intelligence Feeds

The need for high quality cyber threat intelligence to support cyber defense has resulted in a thriving sector of businesses offering specialized intelligence data. What was a relative desert just a few years ago has blossomed into a dynamic market where old providers are struggling to innovate and new entrants are bringing fantastic new capabilities to market. Cyber intelligence is the fastest growing segment in the cyber security market

We provide a list of the cyber intelligence companies we frequently encounter and believe are worthy of consideration in the sources and methods section at the end of the book. We include a list of the top cyber intelligence feeds. Your organization may have already settled on the right ones that meet your mission needs, but there is a good chance not everyone who needs to be getting them is on distribution for them so you may want to check internally. Incident response teams are probably already receiving key feeds, but what about your network operations center or your forensic analysis team? Some feeds might be appropriate for your enterprise risk management function. Executive level reporting from firms may be appropriate for senior executives in your firm. If your organization does not have access to these feeds yet, you can use the list at the end of this report as a starting point in your due diligence on these feeds.

Web intelligence as a source

We believe web intelligence should be considered a special source of information and treated in its own category. It is not the same as the tactical cyber intelligence data feeds you can acquire from feed providers, and is not the same as the data you get from instrumenting your own networks. It is separate and worthy of special consideration as a potential way of gaining ground over some adversaries.

Web Intelligence is the parsing of millions of sources of Internet connected information in a way that is useful to decision-making. It enables the harnessing of Internet sources and adds predictive power to functions such as strategy development, investment decisions and risk assessment/mitigation.

Web Intelligence and Cyber Security

Web Intelligence can enhance enterprise cyber security operations in many ways. It is being used to track vulnerabilities being discussed in hacker channels and exploited in successful attacks. It also provides information on the nature of malicious code and its mitigation strategies. Further, it is a means of tracking the technologies and tactics being employed by attackers, as well as the proven best practices being applied to mitigate threats. It is in this last category of information that web intelligence is making its most unique contributions to cyber defense. Web intelligence is bringing new insights into the identity, motivation and intentions of threat actors, and it is doing so in ways that can contribute to predictions of future behavior.

Since Web Intelligence can provide enhanced information on threat intentions it enables a shifting of cyber defense to more proactive strategies. For example, information on past behaviors of cyber actors associated with real-world events can lead to predictions on future behaviors associated with coming events. This can lead to predictions of when to expect denial of service attacks or when to expect more focused phishing attacks. In some cases it can also lead to predictions on the nature of the deceptive content that can be used in phishing attacks. With more precise insights, action can be taken to mitigate threats before they strike.

Web intelligence also makes important contributions to the issue of assessing who is attacking and why. More refined assessments on this critical element can contribute to assessments of an adversary's next step. Web intelligence can help defenders assess whether an attack is hacktivism or something more sinister. It can also help in assessments of whether or not others will be targets – in particular business partners such as suppliers or customers - and if a more collective defense will need to be mounted.

Web Intelligence can contribute to dedicated cyber security efforts by parsing and correlating millions of data sources relevant to computer security. Succinct articulations of threat actors, their capability, history and intentions can be presented along with dynamically updated information on vulnerabilities and methods required to mitigate vulnerabilities. This can all be presented in conjunction with dynamically updated information on international and regional events that may trigger cyber security events. This automated extraction and presentation of knowledge is already contributing to the situational awareness of several global industries and is now available for general use by cyber defenders in businesses.

Many security professionals we interact with are in the process of enhancing their ability to use web intelligence, and we believe this will be a high growth segment of the security technology portfolio in all major enterprises.

A Strategic Intelligence Assessment

We opened this cyber threat review with an articulation of actors in the following major categories:

- National Governments
- Industrial Spies and Organized Crime Groups
- Terrorists and Extremist Groups
- Hackers and Hacktivists
- Trusted Insiders

Based on the reviews above we can now make some informed projections and assessments on what they may do in the future.

Caution: History has shown us surprise is inevitable, especially since we are dealing with motivated, crafty, dynamic human threats. Still, generic assessments for purposes of discussion can be proposed. Since these are generic assessments, we most definitely recommend a tailoring of the overview below to meet your enterprise needs.

National Governments

National cyber warfare programs pose a unique and powerful threat. Friendly and adversary nations alike seek to acquire a wide range of information from commercial firms, including intellectual property, information on the policies and intent of strategic leadership (for example, selection criteria for new projects), innovation initiatives, and R&D efforts. Countries acting in their own self-interests view cyber as a means to an end and will use cyber conflict capabilities for that purpose.

Nations can bring their intelligence services to bear on this domain. This can be done domestically by targeting foreign companies operating in their country, or by sending intelligence collectors to targeted countries, or co-opting their citizens who travel abroad. Intelligence gathered can be used in secret, or it may be operationalized in order to damage the economy of an adversary country.

An important source of information on the objectives of nations is their stated doctrine and intentions. But even more critical are the direct lessons from actions nations conduct against businesses and other nations and even non-governmental non-profit organizations (NGOs). This information, plus insights from history, can lead to assessments on what they will do next.

National cyber warfare programs are unique in posing a threat along the entire spectrum of objectives that might harm national interests and economic interests (including individual companies). These threats range from propaganda and low-level nuisance web page defacements to espionage and serious disruption with loss of life, to extensive infrastructure disruption. Among the array of cyber threats, only government-sponsored and government encouraged programs are developing the end to end capabilities with the future prospect of causing widespread, long-duration damage to critical infrastructures.

Foreign governments pose a serious and structured threat because they have access to the appropriate technology and are able to enhance the effectiveness of this technology through the use of all source intelligence support, (including penetration of adversaries by traditional agents), extensive funding, and organized professional support. In addition, government agencies may be able to conduct more extensive programs because of their willingness to invest in long-term goals and objectives.

A particularly dangerous threat is the use of a national government to coordinate the actions of criminal groups and hacktivists. This may be a model being employed by both China and Russia today, where both encourage crime when it meets their interests.

Multiple countries have the capability to conduct sustained, high-end cyber attacks against other countries and businesses. Almost every country which has connectivity to the Internet has some ability to conduct cyber attack against businesses.

Cyber security experts and national security thought leaders frequently assert that at this time no nation wants to conduct a military cyber attack directly against the U.S., so they assess the threat as minimal, but we should ask ourselves: what indicators can we observe to determine if and when their intentions change? If you are a leader in a global business and operate in regions where the threat of war exists, you are potentially a direct target by a very high-end adversary. There are methods you can put in place to assess the changing likelihood of this threat (by Cyber I&W), but the best approach here is likely going to be to collaborate with others in your industry or in the region of interest to establish collaborative assessments on events, or outsource to a cyber intelligence firm for this reporting.

Regarding industrial espionage against businesses, clearly this is a problem now. And since these efforts are providing an excellent return on investment so-to-speak, all indications are such attacks will continue. Countries will attack companies to steal intellectual property, including business plans, software, and scientific and technical information. They want what you have and the effort required to steal it is less than the effort required to duplicate it. This should compel businesses to elevate defenses for protecting key intellectual property as well as enhance their ability to collaborate across sectors and to leverage enhanced cyber threat intelligence.

There are many sinister aspects of cyber threats from nation states that go far beyond the scope of this introductory text, and may be best explained by your contacts in the FBI, which underscores the importance of maintaining close relationships there. For purposes of this threat assessment of cyber threats that come from nations we will simply conclude that actual conflict between nations enabled with cyber weapons would be complex, effective, deadly and hard to mitigate for nations and the businesses that operate in them.

Industrial Spies and Organized Crime Groups

Corporate spies and organized crime organizations are threats in cyberspace because of the lucrative payoff they can receive from a successful attack on a corporate network. Criminal groups are known to invest in significant R&D in order to enable attacks.

In two countries in particular, Russia and China, the activities of sophisticated cyber criminals appears to be encouraged when it benefits the goals of the state. This makes for a particularly dangerous combination that puts criminal elements out of reach of Western law enforcement.

Cyber Crime will continue to pose a threat to

companies and to the overall economy through theft of intellectual property and industrial espionage. Organized crime will also continue to invest in botnets of malicious code designed to steal individual financial information for financial motive, and also devise ways to steal from small and medium businesses. This is a multi-billion-dollar market that is only going to get bigger. The big motivator is stealing money from financial and retail organizations.

Rogue corporations also use computer intrusions to tamper with competitors' business proposals, in order to defeat competing bids or unfairly position products in the marketplace. Such behavior hurts not only the losing business but the economy as a whole.

Because cyber criminals' central objectives are to steal, and to avoid getting caught, they are not apt to undertake high-profile operations such as network disruptions. If they do conduct large-scale denial of service attacks, it is usually designed to mask the real reason for their attack.

Terrorists and Extremist Groups

Terrorists have long been known to use IT to

support their operations, and some have begun developing cyber attack capabilities in order to gather intelligence and attack vulnerable targets. Terrorists groups are getting better in this space, with a key example being the Syrian Electronic Army.

Traditional terrorist adversaries of western nations, despite their intentions to damage our physical assets, are less developed in their computer network capabilities and are less inclined to pursue cyber means than are other types of adversaries. They are likely to pose only a limited cyber threat in the next several years. Some adversaries who meet this description may be motivated to act as individuals for a small issue (without higher group sanction). It has long been postulated that cyber attacks may come after a physical attack to interfere with emergency response or to multiply effect in other ways, or prior to a kinetic attack to distract defenders from the real target. These type of attacks can be expected in the future.

Hackers

In the context of the threat, the term Hacker usually implies a person with the ability to gain unauthorized access to computer resources. While some hackers do what they do for personal aggrandizement, increasingly they do it for profit. Most significant, malicious attacks involve hackers operating in groups, often with the backing of organized crime groups and occasionally other nations. Hacktivist groups with geo-political/social agendas (e.g., Anonymous, Lulzsec, AntiSec, etc) are here to stay. When groups of hackers band together their capabilities can become much greater than the sum of their parts.

All indications are that the power of motivated individuals to gain unauthorized access to systems will continue to grow. The sheer numbers of highly skilled, motivated actors means this is a growing threat.

The ability of lone actors to learn from others and become more than just individuals is another cause for concern, especially when there are motivating forces at work. We expect more threats from large collectives of politically motivated hackers. This raises the risk that collectives of individuals acting in a common vector could cause large-scale damage to companies. It was very likely groups of hacktivists who were, perhaps guided by a state, behind massive attacks on Estonia and Georgia in 2007 and 2008. This may have also been how groups are motivated in many of the attacks originating from the PRC.

In summary, collectives of hackers pose significant risk to corporations and this risk will only grow, especially for those corporations that have not established robust cyber intelligence and cyber defense activities.

The Insider Threat:

The malicious insider, by definition, has the credentials of an ordinary employee, and depending on their position or responsibilities, access beyond the ordinary. This access will almost certainly include information on your security policies, in addition to sensitive business information.

It may be that the insider had no malicious intent until something – personal or professional – that triggered a change of outlook or disposition. It is not unheard of for malicious insider to intentionally take a position with a target organization with the intention to cause harm. In the case of the former scenario they usually act alone; in the case of the latter they are likely to be operating as an agent for a third-party: (the aforementioned categories of as actors can also apply to insiders).

Cyber intelligence can inform decisions on insider threats, but this unique threat requires unique information sources, including well-instrumented networks and well-monitored systems inside the enterprise. Cyber intelligence from external sources may also be very relevant. Technology alone will never defeat this type of threat; policy, training and leadership are all required. That said, there are technologies and architectural decisions that can be made that can mitigate damage by insiders while not impeding functionality or utility.

Concluding thoughts

Some things are clear:

- Serious adversaries have goals they are going to fight to achieve. They continue to invest the time and resources necessary to develop the tools and gain the access required to succeed.
- Serious adversaries will not stop until they have achieved their goals, and history suggests that they have a high probability to achieve their goals, eventually.
- A well-instrumented enterprise with a mature cyber intelligence program can detect adversary actions and give you a leg up on mitigating attacks.

Every enterprise will come under attack at some point and your ability to be prepared for probes, insider threats, and malicious attacks will allow your enterprise to continue to function and avoid damage to reputation and business.

Knowledge of threat actors, their attack patterns, and the need for good intelligence on adversaries is available, and it can enhance the decision-making in your organization. It can also inform the rapid tactical action by your security team and can enable automated configuration of your enterprise to mitigate attacks before your adversaries can have an impact.

The attack patterns most noted almost always involve an adversary getting in fast. If you want to develop an ability to find and remove them just as fast you must plan for intelligence support including intelligence support to tactical efforts.

The most prevalent attack patterns are centered on malicious code, errors and their exploitation and then the use of malicious code, at times by insiders. Paying more attention to internal systems can have a big impact on reducing this threat vector.

Only concerted planning efforts will enable the right speed of action. Intelligence on the threat can prove huge in delaying, mitigating and even stopping the bad guys when they get to your enterprise. Knowing what is coming can help slow down the adversary.

Intelligence should inform the policy,

procedures and technologies you put in place to defend your system. This is required so operators can take action based on good intelligence.

Architecting to win requires automation that will allow malware, crimeware, rootkits and implants to be automatically disabled and removed. By building in this automation enterprises can quickly mitigate most threats.

Enhancing Intelligence

Here are key recommendations you can execute on right now to enhance your organization ability to leverage cyber threat intelligence:

1. Conduct an assessment of your own ability to defend, including the maturity of your cyber intelligence activities. Prioritize actions to improve weaknesses discovered in the assessment. Your assessment should help you make hard decisions regarding the right level of resourcing to put on your cyber security and cyber intelligence activities.

2. Stay informed on the threat. The more you know the more you can educate others and the more you can architect to

mitigate the threat. This will also help you decide the right level of resources to apply to address the threat.

3. Seek strategic intelligence threat briefings for yourself and for other senior executives in your organization. This will help more people understand the need to act and will help ensure your cyber defense activities are broadly supported.

4. Understand the information of most importance to your business needs and know where and how it is stored and what protections/controls are placed on the technology that holds this information. Knowing what data is most important to you will help you assess risk and apply greater protections to the most critical components.

5. Assess the state of automation in your enterprise. Few organizations have automated their ability to react to operational and tactical threat indicators. Knowing the state of your enterprise can help you determine next steps.

6. Persistent and continuous threats require constant agility and improvement of defenses. Understand a moving target is harder to hit and architect for continuous improvement in defenses (this is not continuous purchases of the latest tools, tech is just one component of agility).

7. You need to know that no single organization can defend against all attackers. Sophisticated attacks always require secure information sharing and collaboration. Plan for collaboration now.

8. Reach out to other business leaders in your community for discussions on these topics. Help raise the collective awareness of your community and network with others to share lessons learned on business continuity and enterprise risk management associated with cyber security issues.

9. Be prepared for the worst-case scenario and how your enterprise can quickly react to, combat, and contain attacks on your systems. Exercise your cyber incident

response plan.

10. Consider assigning an insider threat manager to assist executives, line of business leaders and technologists in mitigating the threat from malicious insiders.

Appendix 1: History of the Cyber Threat

What follows is a brief outline of cyber security history and the critical lessons they provide:

Aug 1986: Hanover Hackers/Cuckoo's Egg

Penetrations into U.S. sites discovered by Lawrence Berkeley National Lab researcher Clifford Stoll led to the first major national and international forensic investigation of a cyber attack. The lessons learned in this thrilling case make this a critical incident to study for all cyber defenders.

Lessons for today: Well-instrumented systems can detect and help defend against attackers. Collaboration among defenders is critical.

Nov 1988: The Morris Worm

The Morris Worm propagated throughout internetworked systems including those of the federal government. The aftermath saw the establishment of computer response organizations throughout the

Department of Defense and increased funding for computer security research provided to academic institutions. The Computer Emergency Response Team (CERT) at Carnegie Mellon University was funded.

Lesson for today: Think through who you will need to collaborate with outside your organizations and how you will do that if your communications are attacked. Exercise this collaboration!

1998: Solar Sunrise

The Solar Sunrise attackers penetrated over 500 servers and operated in a way as to lead senior defense decision-makers to suspect an organized adversary (possibly Iraq) was involved. In the end, three teenaged hackers, including an Israeli, were charged. This activity resulted in increased funding to cyber defense organizations and the creation of a new joint military activity called the "Joint Task Force Computer Network Defense" or JTF-CND (the Author was first JTF-CND Director of Intelligence (J2)).

Lessons for today: Think through the

governance process of your incident response efforts. Ensure your systems are patched in a timely and comprehensive manner.

1998: Moonlight Maze

Many believe this was a Russian state sponsored cyber intelligence operation. Targets included the Departments of Defense and Energy as well as many businesses. It resulted in enhanced counterintelligence resources and more information sharing across the law enforcement, counterintelligence and computer incident response communities.

Lesson for today: Understand that when a well-resourced adversary wants something they will keep trying till they get it. Know there will be limits to what international law enforcement can do for you.

2000: Maroochy Shire Sewage Management Attacks

This attack is notable as being the first known

cyber attack against civilian infrastructure that caused real physical damage. An Australian man hacked a computerized waste management system and caused millions of liters of raw sewage to spill out into local parks, rivers and even the grounds of a Hyatt Regency hotel.

Lessons for Today: This proved the theoretical attack of cyber against physical systems was possible, raising questions about what attacks on hospitals, power plants and other key infrastructure might look like.

2007: Cyber Attacks On Estonia

Beginning in April 2007 the country of Estonia was subjected to a massive cyber attack which included denial of service attacks against infrastructure and banking, defacing of websites and news outlets, and attacks against government organizations. Russia was accused of having direct involvement, though no definitive proof of this exists.

Lessons for Today: The "who" does not matter if they are getting results. Place an emphasis on attack mitigation and response in order to weather the storm. And understand the geopolitical connections to cyber activities.

2007: Escalation of Attacks from China

It is hard to pin a date on when cyber espionage from China really escalated, but detection and reporting certainly escalated in 2007. During a December 2007 trip to Beijing, spyware designed to extract key information from computers was noted on all the laptops of the Department of Commerce delegation, including devices used by Commerce Secretary Carlos Gutierrez. Access to such data would have given the PRC delegation access to key policy documents including information on U.S. positions on intellectual property rights, market access and consumer product safety.

Lessons for today: Do not expect nation's to play by your standards or to act like you would. Also know that overseas travel is an especially vulnerable time and requires special protections.

2008: Buckshot Yankee

This involved what could have been a foreign power using malicious software (malware) with an objective of extracting information from U.S. military networks (including classified networks). Although there are no indications this activity was successful the sophisticated technology could have worked and is a very real threat to even "air gapped" networks. This activity resulted in more awareness and more funding for cyber security throughout the federal government, but still similar issues continue today. Note that the penetration method was designed to exploit business processes put in place by operational forces trying to make IT better serve their missions.

Lesson for today: Understand that technologies used in any enterprise will continually change, and with each new change comes potentially new attack vectors.

2008: Cyber Attacks On Georgia

In attacks analogous to those against Estonia,

key sites in Georgia were attacked, this time in conjunction with Russian forces invading Georgia. Cyber attack and cyber espionage is now an integral part of many nation's military planning. It is the rule not the exception.

Lesson for Today: Always expect cyber activity coincident with military activity.

2008: Cyber Attack Causes Turkey Pipeline Explosion

Reporting by Bloomberg investigators in 2014 indicate an August 2008 pipeline explosion in Refahiye Turkey was caused by a cyber attack, with great circumstantial evidence pointing to a Russian attack. This is currently the first use of cyber attack for a major infrastructure attack.

Lessons for today: The economic impact of this explosion went far beyond the region and show a very real threat to infrastructures.

2009: GhostNet

Uncovered by researchers at Information Warfare Monitor and SecDev Group. This activity was large-scale cyber espionage with command and control based in China. Political opponents of PRC were among targets. Infiltrations were successfully executed against high-value political, economic, media locations, embassies, businesses in 103 countries.

Lessons for today: When a powerful adversary wants to get in nothing will stop them, you will need to defeat them after breach. And good people can be deceived into clicking links.

2010: Google Aurora Attacks

This attack was most closely associated with Google due to their leading role in publicly denouncing the role of the Chinese government, but many other companies were also attacked in this same intrusion set. A key goal of the attack was to gain access to and potentially modify source code repositories at high tech, security and defense contractor firms.

Lessons for today: Understand that in some cases countries where U.S. companies might be doing business can be complicit in attacks. And remember that your most precious business assets deserve special protections.

2010: Stuxnet

This computer worm was discovered in June 2010. It was designed to attack industrial systems that allow automation of electromechanical processes. These systems are known as Programmable Logic Controllers or PLCs. In this case, the PLCs were associated with centrifuges in Iran designed to enhance nuclear material. But as a category of devices, PLCs are widely deployed to control machinery in factory assembly lines. Stuxnet was designed to enable itself to propagate across networks and boundaries including by use of unwitting insiders who use media between networks.

Lessons for today: Be very suspicious when someone tells you that an "air gapped" system is defended from malicious code. It may be, but then again, it might not be. Verify what protections are in place and prepare to respond to breach.

2011: Operation Shady RAT

Reported in 2011 but forensics indicated had been underway since at least 2006. Over 70 organizations were hit, including defense contractors, businesses worldwide, the United Nations, International Olympic Committee.

Lesson for today: Collaborative intelligence work by good guys can help mitigate threats.

2011: Wikileaks

This unauthorized disclosure of large quantities of material resulted in significant activities and planning across the federal space aimed at enhancing security of information from disclosure.

Lesson for today: Find balance between information sharing and data protection, and understand the human element in protecting data.

2011: RSA Attacks

Intruders managed to infiltrate one of the world's top cyber security companies and stole data that could impair their core security products, including some used by over 40 million businesses to keep networks safe. Methods were similar to the Aurora attacks, and like many others, began with a phishing email.

Lessons for today: Like many other cases, a group that should have had access to all the defensive capabilities industry could muster neglected to defend what was important to them. Every enterprise should understand, if you or your people develop hubris and think you will not be attacked, you will almost certainly be proven wrong. Approach the cyber threat with humility and respect.

Sep 2012: Saudi ARAMCO:

In one of the most destructive attacks noted against any company to date, Saudi state-owned oil company ARAMCO had data destroyed on over 3/4 of their companies computers (reports indicate up to 30,000 computers were destroyed). Indications are that the threat actors were very sophisticated both technically and in their understanding of the cultural dynamics of the organization.

Lesson for today: Understand that destruction of physical infrastructure by cyber attack is not just a theoretical possibility.

Jan 2013: New York Times

New York Times acknowledged hacks into its papers by Chinese sources.

Lessons for today: It is interesting that some of the best reporting on the cyber threat was coming from the New York Times. But it did not mean they were taking their own warnings seriously. Never assume anyone is defended.

2012: Operation Cleaver

The highly regarded research team at Cylance provided a well documented report Iran positioning for offensive cyber attack on western infrastructure. Reported in 2014, forensics indicate the attacks and sinister positioning for offensive cyber war have been underway since 2012.

Lesson for Today: Countries are planning to use cyber attacks as strategic weapons. Businesses should understand they may need to operate in environments of cyber conflict.

Jan 2013: US Banks Attacked

A perpetual problem, attacks on US banks accelerated during this period, including very large-scale attacks meant to overwhelm system capacity (Denial of Service attacks) as well as attempts to penetrate systems.

Lesson for today: Understand that even relatively well-defended enterprises can fall victim to a dedicated and well-resourced attacker.

Feb 2013: US Federal Reserve Hacked

The group Anonymous attacks against Federal

Reserve investigated by FBI. Attackers compromised data from the Fed's Emergency Communications System.

Lesson for today: Test your assumptions: just because you think something should be well defended does not mean it is. And exercise leadership in remediation and mitigation, even if only in training.

Feb 2013 The Mandiant Report Released

Computer security company Mandiant released a report exposing one of China's Cyber Espionage Groups. This report, widely considered one of the best articulations of the threat, resulted in significant positive awareness on the seriousness of the threat. It generated new levels of conversations on the high end cyber threat.

Lessons for today: Understand the potential resources that could be behind attacks on your enterprise. Also understand the potential power of collaborating with others to support collective defense.

March 2013: DarkSeoul

In March 2013 three South Korean television stations, several banks and large numbers of ATM machines came under attack. The attack used infrastructures commonly used by both North Korea and China for cyber attacks, with most researchers concluding that this was a North Korean sponsored event.

Lessons for today: It can be very hard to attribute attacks, and even after you do it can be hard to do anything about it. The best policy is to have solid defenses for any infrastructure you operate.

June 2013: The Snowden Leaks

The ability of a single person to take so many documents would be hard to believe just a few years ago.

Lessons for today: Organizations should instrument their enterprises to prevent, monitor and if required mitigate against legitimate-but-malicious insiders. Understand that process and policy are also critical for defense.

Throughout 2013 and 2014:

There have been a numbing amount of intrusions into retail and finance and ecommerce sites and very high profile attacks against individuals in the entertainment and government sectors. Successful attacks have occurred against some of the largest, best protected institutions, including JP Morgan, whose CEO stated that they spend about $200 million per year to defend against attacks and that would soon increase to $250 million. Famous name retailers like Home Depot, Target and Staples have suffered great losses and found that there were things they wish they would have done better.

Lessons for today: Understand, history is not over. Cyber-attacks are perpetual events not rare occurrences.

Nov and Dec 2014: Sony Attacks

The ongoing attacks into Sony have been a watershed event for many reasons. One is it captured the attention of the public and maintained that attention through several news cycles, something unheard of in the world of cyber security. As of the time of this writing this is still an active investigation, but the FBI has already publicly announced that North Korea is behind these attacks.

Lessons for today: It is critically important that firms in all sectors of the economy evaluate their security posture, find gaps and mitigate them. It is also important to have a plan in place to respond to breach.

Dec 2014: German Steel Mill

The German Federal Office for Information Security reported an attack against an unnamed steel mill initiated by a phishing attack that led to manipulation of an destruction of control systems and significant damage to blast furnaces.

Lesson: Attacks on physical plants will soon be the new norm.

Appendix 2: Sources and Methods

We track publicly available information on the threat on a daily basis and maintain updated threat assessments at our CTOvision.com site based on open source information on reported breaches. We also provide automated feeds on open source threat information at our TheCyberThreat.com site. Both these sites are key references for this study.

We also stay very close to elements of the operational cyber security community and learn what we can from the people directly engaged in enterprise cyber defense of governments and corporations.

More Reading:

There are many other key sources that have informed and influenced the views of the threat articulated here. Links to all of these are available at TheCyberThreat.com

These are some we recommend you examine to dive deeper into the nature of the threat:

The Cuckoo's Egg: Exciting first person account of Cliff Stoll's tracking of a cyber spy. The story here is nearly identical to the tactics used by many adversaries today. This is the next book you should read if you have not already.

The yearly Verizon Data Breach Investigations Report: Insights from a growing community of cyber defenders

The Cyber Council of the Intelligence and National Security Alliance (INSA): Providing white papers and studies on cyber intelligence

The Feb 2013 APT1 report by Mandiant: Important details of one of many actors in cyberspace.

A Fierce Domain: Conflict In Cyberspace: The definitive work on cyber history.

Cyber Adversary Characterization: A key reference for technical defenders that helped ensure our head was on right. We recommend it for the more technically inclined.

Research Notes of Sam Liles on Security,

Privacy, Insider Threats and Espionage:
Tremendous reference.

The Insider Threat focus area of the CERT CC:
Studies on elements of insider threat very
useful for defenders

Cyberpower and National Security: Great
insights into the potential for state on state
cyber actions.

Information Warfare: The first edition of this
book by Winn Schwartau started many of us
thinking about the threat. The new edition
continues to bring lessons on the threat
relevant for corporations and governments.

Operation Cleaver: Cylance details evidence
and assessments indicating Iranian sponsored
organizations are using cyber to prepare for
strategic attack.

Cyber Intelligence Sources

If you are looking seeking sources of cyber
threat intelligence to enhance the defense of your

business you now have a wide range of providers to chose from. If you already have a managed service provider you probably already have access to a great deal of external data. Many vendors also supply data to support their technologies. And a large number of firms have stood up to provide data that is interoperable with corporate systems and processes.

Below we list key ones to consider (links to all these are available at TheCyberThreat.com):

- AlienVault.com: Multiple sources including large honeynets that profile adversaries.

- CrowdStrike.com: Advanced threat intel as part of their threat protection platform.

- Cyveilance.com: Unique feeds on threat actors: indications of criminal intent.

- EmergingThreats.net: A variety of feeds.

- FireEye.com: DTI- Dynamic Threat Intelligence service.

- FusionX.com: Strategic insights, high end analysis and defensive measures.

- HackSurfer.com (SurfWatch): Insights tailored to your business.

- HexisCyber.com: Feed supports automated actions.

- InternetIdentity.com: Threat feeds from their big data solution ActiveTrust.

- iSightPartners.com: ThreatScape series.

- LookingGlass.com: Maps of infrastructure, connectivity and ownership, plus threat intelligence.

- MalwareDomains.com: A list of domains known to be associated with Malware.

- RecordedFuture.com: Organizes information from the Internet.

- RedSkyAlliance.com and WapackLabs.com: Information sharing and intelligence, led by operationally-focused leaders with proven past performance, now serving large, medium and small organizations.

- SecureWorks.com: Provides feeds and also instruments networks.

- Symantec.com: DeepInsight feeds on a variety of topics including reputation.

- Team-Cymru.com: Threat intelligence plus bogon lists.

- ThreatBrief.com: The Daily Threat Brief

provides context for executives

- ThreatConnect.com by Cyber Squared. Focused on information sharing.

- ThreatGrid.com: Unified malware analysis. Now part of Cisco.

- ThreatStop.com: Block Botnets by IP reputation.

- ThreatStream.com: Famous team. Multiple sources in interoperable platform.

We regard the following as the most important government sources of Cyber Threat Intelligence:

- The Defense Cyber Crime Center (DC3): Providing daily context on the cyber threat and incidents via newsletter and their Twitter feed.

- US Computer Emergency Response Team (US-CERT): Responds to major incidents and analyzes threats. Shares information on vulnerabilities via alerts and announcements. Large body of tips and awareness items useful to your cyber threat intelligence program.

- European Union Agency for Network and Information Security (ENISA): Tremendous references, publications, media.

- <u>FBI Cyber Crime</u>: News on latest cases plus testimony of FBI seniors to Congress on cybercrime topics.

  <u>StopThinkConnect</u>: Not much operational, but good background for the workforce. Striving to make cyber security understandable by people. Good tips for corporate and personal awareness programs.

About the Author

The author of this summary is Bob Gourley, a former government CTO and former leader of intelligence support to cyber defense for the DoD. Bob is the publisher of CTOvision.com and a partner at Cognitio Corp. At Cognitio, Bob leads research and analysis activities, due diligence assessments and strategic consulting and participates in enterprise cyber security reviews for our corporate clients.

Bob is a founding member and member of the board of directors of the Cyber Conflict Studies Association (CCSA), a non-profit group focused on enhancing the study of cyber conflict at leading academic institutions and furthering the ability of the nation to understand the complex dynamics of conflict in cyberspace.

Bob serves on public boards and advisory boards for a number of companies including Centripetal Networks, Haystax, Wayin, Invincea, Spacecurve, Optensity and Triumfant. He has advised Cloudera, Pentaho, Platfora and Recorded Future. He is also on the Cyber Council of the non-profit Intelligence and National Security Alliance (INSA). Bob is also on several government advisory boards.

Acknowledgements

Deep insights into strategic, operational and tactical cyber threats, approaches to enhance cyber intelligence, and critical comments on this report were provided by John Campbell, Matt Devost, Michael Tanji, Harry Raduege, Michael McConnell, Bill Studeman, Rich Haver, Jason Healey, Jeff Stutzman, Jim Longly, Robert Rodriguez, John Felker, Keith Alexander, Michael Hayden, Sam Liles, Richard Schaeffer and Nick Lantuh. Several corporate CISOs and CTOs and senior government executives also offered comments but asked to remain unnamed. Still they are very much appreciated.

Contributions were made by the founding partners of Cognitio: Bob Flores, a former government CTO and architect with experience designing systems made to withstand sophisticated attack, Roger Hockenberry, a noted cyber security professional and former CTO and partner at Gartner who focuses on sophisticated network defense solutions, and David Highnote, one of the nation's great business technologists known for making rapid contributions to enterprise security programs. All of our partners at Cognitio are very active in conducting cyber security assessments in industry and government.

Disclaimer to meet pre-publication review requirements: The views expressed in this work are those of the author and do not reflect the official policy or position of the U.S. Government, the Department of Defense, or any of its components.

CPSIA information can be obtained at www.ICGtesting.com
Printed in the USA
BVOW08s1931170315

392108BV00012BA/142/P